THE 30-DAY MUSIC
WRITING CHALLENGE

THE 30-DAY MUSIC WRITING CHALLENGE

ED BELL

Bell, Ed
Book : The 30-Day Music Writing Challenge

Library of Congress Control Number: 2019910030

ISBN 978-0-9981302-5-5 (Paperback edition)

Published September 2019
New York City

CONTENTS

ABOUT THE SONG FOUNDRY

At The Song Foundry it's our mission to share great songwriting ideas with the world. At thesongfoundry.com we publish articles about songwriting, host free videos on various songwriting topics, and offer Skype songwriting coaching worldwide.

Connect with us online to find out more:

thesongfoundry.com

youtube.com/TheSongFoundry

facebook.com/TheSongFoundry

twitter.com/TheSongFoundry

ALSO AVAILABLE

The 30-Day Lyric Writing Challenge

The 30-Day Creativity Challenge

The 30-Day Speed Songwriting Challenge

Find out more about all of the 30-Day Challenges at
thesongfoundry.com/30-day-challenges

INTRODUCTION: LET'S GET WRITING

Hello – and welcome. You have in your hands a month of stimulating and powerful challenges that are going to get you writing music for songs smarter, faster and bolder.

As you might know, the only way to become a better songwriter is to write a lot – and that's exactly what these challenges will help you do. And best of all, you can complete them in any musical style or genre you like, and with whatever instruments, technology and/or voices you have at your disposal.

So let's talk about how it all works.

The challenges are designed for you to work through in 30 days, in as little as 15 minutes per day. Of course, if you're extra keen you could do the challenges in less time, or if you're extra busy you could spread them over a longer period of time – but 30 days is a great schedule to stick to if it works for you.

There are two types of challenges in this book. The first ten – spread over ten days – are quick 15-minute challenges that will have you creating and rewriting things like grooves, chord progressions and melodies.

The second ten – spread over twenty days – have you working on more substantial projects, which are designed to take anywhere from 30 minutes to an hour, depending on how much time you need, want and/or have available. You'll get two days to finish each of these – and you'll probably get the best results if you do them in one sitting then take a day off, but you could split each challenge over two days if you'd rather.

If you've taken either *The 30-Day Lyric Writing Challenge* or *The 30-Day Creativity Challenge*, you'll realize this is a slightly different format. In fact, while the key to finishing those challenges is sticking religiously to a 10-minute timeslot each day, with these challenges if it takes you 5 or 10 minutes longer than the official time to do them justice, you should definitely take the extra time and live with no regrets. (Especially around Days 8 to 10, where you might find a few more minutes really helpful.)

Add five minutes to read and understand each challenge before you start, and that's pretty much all the time you'll need to get through them.

Exactly when you do the challenges is up to you – but, like always, I recommend you commit to a plan before you start to maximize your chances of getting through all 30 days. (Again, if the only way to get better at songwriting is practice, then consistency – and a regular schedule, if you can commit to one – is really important.)

All of the challenges help you practice the real-life skills songwriters have to master to create bold, distinctive and well-crafted songs. They're not drills or exercises – they're genuine, real-life challenges that will help you develop skills you'll be able to use in everything you write – whatever level of experience you're working at right now. And to help you put each challenge in context, they all come with a gray 'Why it matters' box, which will help clarify how each challenge is part of the bigger picture of writing music for songs.

As I said, all of the challenges are open-ended enough that you can complete them in any style or genre you like, using whatever instruments, technology and level of experience you have. That said, you will get more out the challenges if you can read music notation.

I know – being able to read music as a songwriter is definitely optional. (There are plenty of über successful songwriters who say they can't.) But it's a skill that's definitely worth investing in even to a basic level, if you can.

Anyway, in the meantime you'll still get plenty out of these challenges whether you read music or not. In fact, if you don't, there are downloadable audio recordings that go with all of the challenges that involve reading music notation and where you might want reassurance you've read them correctly – even if you read music well.

Those challenges are marked with a little headphones symbol just after the challenge number, and you can get your hands on all of the accompanying audio recordings from The Song Foundry site at **thesongfoundry.com/music-challenge**.

As well as using whatever instruments or technology you like to work through the challenges, it's totally up to you to use whatever working methods or processes that work for you. If you write at the piano, that's great. If you write holding a guitar, that's great. If you write in a DAW – a Digital Audio Workstation like Cubase, Logic or GarageBand – that's great. If you like to sing and jump around the room while you complete each challenge, that's great too.

However you write, one thing that's going to be important is that you record what you create for each challenge somehow. That might be on paper, it might be on a hard drive, it might be in a voicenote on your phone or on some other recording device. You'll definitely want a record of everything you create in case you want to use those ideas later in real-life songs, but also because you're going to reuse some of the material you create in earlier challenges as you progress through this book.

Oh, and while we're here, there's one specific thing you should start preparing for before you reach the final challenge. I know, it's a while away, but as Louis Pasteur said, "Fortune favors a prepared mind". (I'm sure this was explicitly what he was taking about.)

Anyway, your final challenge is going to be a cover challenge – an opportunity to write a creative new version of one of your favorite songs. So you'll need to have a song picked out – and unless you know it from memory, a copy of either the sheet music or just the lyric and chords – before then.

Finally, because this is a book about writing music and talking about writing music sometimes gets technical, there are three appendixes at the back of the book you should know about before you dive in.

Appendix 1 is a rundown of the twelve major and minor triads (chords) you might use while tackling these challenges – as well as the guitar chord charts that show you how to play them.

Appendix 2 is a summary of how verse-chorus structures work in songwriting, taken from my book *The Art of Songwriting*, if you want to brush up on that.

Appendix 3 is a short glossary of all of the important musical terminology you'll find in this book – in case you come across any words you're not sure about.

Depending on your level of experience and/or understanding of music theory, you may or may not need these appendixes – that's why they're appendixes – but they're there if you do.

All that covered, you're pretty much ready to go.

So let's get writing.

[DAY 1]
THREE UPBEAT GROOVES

[DAY 1]

THREE UPBEAT GROOVES

A song's groove – the core instrumental ideas or figuration that define its feel or vibe – is like its heartbeat. It's a big part of what gives a song its character and what lets it bring its lyric and message to life in a deep and instinctual way.

That means that art of writing great grooves isn't just about the notes, rhythms and instrumentation that make up its music – it's also about the overall mood or emotions the groove creates, and how that matches and supports the song's lyric.

So today, with that in mind, you're going to spend fifteen minutes coming up with three upbeat grooves you could use in a song's verse or chorus.

Why it matters: Coming up with interesting, evocative and distinctive grooves is one of the most important skills every songwriter has to master.

DAY 1 CHALLENGE

 15 mins

Come up with <u>three different upbeat grooves</u>.

As I said in the introduction, you can write in whatever musical styles or genres you like, using whatever tools – guitar, piano, a Digital Audio Workstation, whatever – you have at your disposal.

Each groove can be as short as a single measure – and probably no longer than four – and could be as simple as strummed or repeated chords, or something more intricate or developed if you like.

Whatever you choose, you're trying to create three grooves that would sound at home in an upbeat song's verse or chorus. (For the record, 'upbeat' could refer to tempo or mood or both – it's your call.)

For today, it's fine to repeat the groove over a single chord, like C major. You're going to think about spreading grooves out to fill full sections later, but in this challenge your focus is on coming up with textures, sounds and/or chord figurations that aim to capture a specific feel, character or mood.

If that takes you way less than fifteen minutes, spend the rest of the time either writing more grooves or refining and developing your first three ideas.

[DAY 2]
FOUR-CHORD
PROGRESSIONS

[DAY 2]

FOUR-CHORD PROGRESSIONS

Four-bar, four-chord progressions are a staple of songwriting. They tend to be really effect because they're compact enough to be simple but long enough that repeating them over and over again doesn't get boring.

Plus, because they're so compact, crafting interesting and distinctive four-chord progressions is usually pretty straightforward – even if you don't have tons of music theory knowledge. So that's what you're going to practice today.

Why it matters: Four-chord progressions are important in virtually all genres of songwriting, so being able to come up with your own is an essential songwriting skill.

DAY 2 CHALLENGE

 15 mins

Find at least four effective four-chord progressions.

Each progression can be made up of any four chords you like – and in some of the progressions you may end up including the same chord more than once. Be as adventurous with the chords you choose as you like – but if you're not sure where to start, stick to the chords C, Dm, F, G and Am, and see what you can create with them.

Whatever chords you use, your goal is to create a feeling of movement, some kind of cycle or miniature journey through your choice of chords – that's why they're called chord progressions and not successions.

Play around, try different combinations and see what gives a sense of progression or a gentle rise and fall that you like the sound of. When trying out different progressions it's fine to use either a simple strumming pattern or held chords – don't spend tons of time turning them into specific grooves.

If you come up with four interesting progressions and have time to spare, try to come up with more.

[DAY 3]
MELODY
CHALLENGE #1

[DAY 3]

MELODY CHALLENGE #1

So far we've focused on a song's supporting acts – its groove and chord progressions – but today we're going center stage and thinking about vocal melodies.

A great vocal melody, or topline, is one of the most important parts of a great song. For starters, it's part of what makes a song memorable and catchy – it's much easier to remember words set to music than just words on their own. The vocal melody is also part of what gives a song its character or feel.

Great melodic writing is all about artful repetition – about repeating melodic units or building blocks called motifs to craft melodies that are at least coherent and satisfying, and at best irresistible. So that's what you're going to be thinking about today.

Why it matters: Great melodic writing is one of the most important songwriting skills – both for making your song memorable and using its melody to help conjure up a specific mood or vibe.

DAY 3 CHALLENGE

15 mins

Write <u>an 8- or 16-bar chorus melody</u> that starts like this:

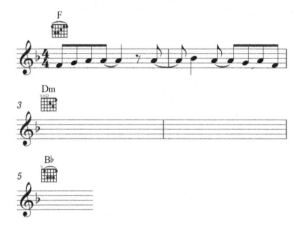

As I said, the key to great melodic writing is using repetition to create a coherent overall effect. In this case, the simplest thing you can do is to repeat the first two measures three times over and write two final measures to round things off into an 8-bar melody – and you might be surprised by how good that sounds.

But if you can, there's plenty of room to be more adventurous. Try playing around with the two main melodic motifs in the measures you've got – the first four-note figure and the off-beat six-note figure after it – to see if you can repeat and/or develop those motifs into a melody that sounds good to you. An 8-bar melody is fine, or you could write a 16-bar melody for a slightly tougher challenge.

[DAY 4]
THREE RHYTHMIC
GROOVES

[DAY 4]

THREE RHYTHMIC GROOVES

One of the things that most characterizes a song's groove is its rhythm. On-beat rhythms usually sound plain, emotional or elegant. Syncopated, off-beat rhythms tend to sound fresh, funky and even seductive. Sparse rhythms sound open and calm, and busy rhythms often sound lively, energetic or intense.

So in today's challenge you'll get three specific but contrasting 4/4 rhythms – with no pitches or anything else attached – and it's up to you to turn them into fully fleshed-out grooves.

> **Why it matters:** A groove's rhythm is one of its most defining characteristics, so starting with a rhythmic idea is a great way to generate effective new grooves.

DAY 4 CHALLENGE

⏱ **15 mins**

Create <u>three different grooves</u> that use each of these rhythms somewhere:

Like with all of the challenges, you can create grooves in any genre or style you want – though the rhythms might draw you to certain genres more strongly than others. You'll also have to pick a tempo for each of them, based on what suits each rhythm.

How you use the rhythms is entirely up to you – they could become parts of drum tracks, strumming patterns on guitar, broken chord patterns on keys. The simplest way to use each rhythm is to put it in a single part, instrument or track – though you could split them between two or more parts. But again, it's not just about the details – it's also about the overall vibe or feel each groove creates.

Like always, if you want to draw the groove out over two or four different chords you can, but figuring out the groove over a single chord is fine too.

[DAY 5]
16-BAR CHORD
PROGRESSION

[DAY 5]

16-BAR CHORD PROGRESSION

On Day 2, you came up with a handful of effective four-bar chord progressions. Today you're going to take things to the next level by creating a 16-bar progression.

The good news is that 16-bar progressions aren't four-bar progressions made four times as difficult. With longer progressions there's usually plenty of repetition of the chords within them – just like the melodic repetition we talked about on Day 3. So the key to today's challenge isn't just to come up with chords but to craft a chord sequence that has enough sense of balance, structure and symmetry to work as a whole.

Why it matters: While four-chord progressions are a really effective songwriting tool, it's also useful to be able to craft longer and more sophisticated progressions when you want to.

DAY 5 CHALLENGE

 15 mins

Extend these chords into a 16-bar chord progression:

| C | Dm | F | G | |

As you know by now, the key to completing this challenge is to make sure the 16 measures you come up with include plenty of repetition – either identical repetitions or with some variation.

In fact, I recommend you think of the progression as four 4-bar units and try to build plenty of repetition between those units. Here are two common schemes you can use if you like:

1) AAA'B: Repeat measures 1–4 identically in measures 5–8, then again (maybe with some variation) in measures 9–12. Then write new chords for measures 13–16 that feel like some kind of extension or continuation of measures 9–12.

2) ABAB or ABAC: Extend measures 1–4 into a complete 8-bar progression. Then either repeat that exactly in measures 9–16, or (more fun) copy measures 1–4 into measures 9–12 but write new chords in measures 13–16.

As usual, play around and see what sounds good to you – whether you use either of these schemes or not – and feel free to use chords that are as simple or complex as you like.

Finally, because this progression is in C major, to give it a sense of completion you'll probably want to finish off on a plain C chord.

[DAY 6]
THE COUNTERPOINT
CHALLENGE

[DAY 6]

THE COUNTERPOINT CHALLENGE

Counterpoint is all about the relationship between two or more melodic lines. And good counterpoint is all about creating interesting relationships between those melodic lines – making sure they work together well but are also interesting and coherent on their own.

In songwriting, the most important counterpoint is usually between your vocal melody and your song's bass line. It might sound weird to think of your bass as a melody, but since it's the harmonic foundation the rest of your song sits on – the lowest note in the texture – it's a good idea to be aware of the relationship it has with your song's most prominent melodic part: its vocal melody.

Generally, you want the two voices to form an interesting partnership or dialogue – and that's the focus for today's challenge.

Why it matters: All great music relies on good counterpoint – making sure the individual voices fit together well – but in songwriting this is especially important between your vocal melody and bassline.

DAY 6 CHALLENGE

🕐 **15 mins**

Rewrite this vocal melody and/or bass line to improve the counterpoint between the two lines:

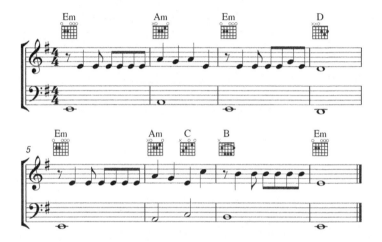

While this melody might look OK at first glance, if you play or sing it over the bass line you'll realize it kind of sucks. The vocal melody has the exact same shape as the bass, and it's mostly just the bass note two octaves higher – so it doesn't sound very interesting.

So in rewriting, try to make the two parts or 'voices' more independent, but still complementary. In particular, try to make the two parts pair up more on different notes – use a different chord note in the melody than the bass – and make the parts move more independently and more in contrary motion – in opposite directions.

To do that, you can change any part of the vocal melody or the bass line – including the chords – or both.

23

[DAY 7]
THREE SLOW GROOVES

[DAY 7]

THREE SLOW GROOVES

Today you've got your final simple groove writing challenge. And to mix things up a bit, you're going to be coming up with slower grooves you could use in a more emotional and expressive – or at least more chilled out – song.

As always, you can write in whatever styles and genres you like, but slower grooves tend to give you more opportunity to craft something extra detailed so it's worth taking advantage of that.

Why it matters: Having the versatility to write grooves in a range of styles, depending on what each song calls for, is a really useful skill as a songwriter.

DAY 7 CHALLENGE

 15 mins

Come up with <u>three different slow grooves</u>.

As I said, one of the fun challenges with slower grooves is that they often give you more room — literally and metaphorically — to create music that's more intricate or detailed. So today you can think especially hard about the details you could include in the figuration, rhythms and instrumentation and the overall emotion or mood they create.

This time, feel free to spread each groove out over a few different chords — pick one of the progressions you came up with on Day 2 if you like — but if you'd rather keep them to a single chord, that's fine too.

[DAY 8]
VERSE AND CHORUS CHORD PROGRESSION

[DAY 8]

VERSE AND CHORUS CHORD PROGRESSION

Today you've got another chord writing challenge and you've got a whole 32 measures to play with, split between a verse and chorus of 16 measures each.

Writing effective chord progressions isn't just about filling space and time with chords that sort of, kind of work. The chords you use can also play an important role in marking out your song's structure – both in the way the chord progressions of each section contrast, and the way you can use harmony, for example, to make the end of your verse sound more restless and unsettled and the end of your chorus more settled and complete.

So in this challenge you're going to try putting that idea into practice, and craft chords that would fit an entire verse-chorus cycle in a song.

> **Why it matters:** The chords you choose can be one of the most important ways you mark out your song's individual sections and overall structure.

DAY 8 CHALLENGE

 15 mins

Complete these verse and chorus chord progressions:

VERSE

Am		G		C				

CHORUS

C		C/B		Am		G	
				C			

One of the keys here is to use plenty of repetition like you did on Day 5. Another is to choose chords that lead and build into the chorus – the end of the verse should feel like it's punctuated with a colon – then write chords that make the chorus sound complete at the end – like a period or full stop.

Use whatever knowledge of harmony you have combined with plenty of trial and error to figure out what sounds good to you. As a reminder, slash chords – like C/B – indicate a chord with a different bass note than usual – like C major over a B bass.

[DAY 9]
MELODY
CHALLENGE #2

[DAY 9]

MELODY CHALLENGE #2

Next up, it's another melody writing challenge, only from a different angle – today you're concentrating on writing a melody that would be at home in a song's verse.

All of the ideas about repetition and development of motifs that you put into practice on Day 3 still apply here. But while chorus melodies tend to be more declarative and expressive – and melodic – you usually find most verse melodies are more speech-like, even conversational, and in a lower register, or part of the voice. That's one of the ways a verse-chorus structure makes its chorus feel like the song's main event, while making its verses set up each chorus and anticipate the moments they arrive.

Like everything in songwriting, there are always exceptions, but this is an important principle to bear in mind as you create the vocal melodies for the various sections in a song.

Why it matters: One important way you can differentiate your song's sections is through the character of their vocal melodies.

DAY 9 CHALLENGE

Write <u>an 8- or 16-bar verse melody</u> that starts like this:

Again, the key is to create a melody that includes plenty of repetition. To me, there are three motifs you can play with in the two measures you're given — the repeated note figure in the first half of measure 1, the syncopated figure in the second half of measure 1, and the three-note idea in measure 2 — but this time you could also introduce one or more of your own motifs.

If you decide to write a 16-bar melody, you can repeat the chords I've given you an extra time, or write your own if you'd rather.

[DAY 10]
THE PROSODY
CHALLENGE

[DAY 10]

THE PROSODY CHALLENGE

Today it's your final shorter challenge and it's a good one: a challenge devoted to the art of prosody – the art of combining a lyric and vocal melody into a seamless whole.

In short, prosody is about making sure your vocal melody delivers its lyric clearly and in a way that more or less resembles natural speech. That usually comes down to three fundamental things:

First, it means making sure the natural word stresses in a lyric match the rhythmic stresses in the music – that you don't put the em-PHA-sis on the wrong syl-LAB-ble.

Second, it means making the lyric's rhythm feel like a reasonable representation of the way you'd speak those words in real life – or at least not a distortion of it.

And third, it means using high or long notes to emphasize the more meaningful words in your lyric, and not giving insignificant words like 'the' or 'and' a weird melodic or rhythmic emphasis.

Why it matters: Prosody – combining lyrics and music effectively – is a subtle but essential part of crafting songs that are compelling and easy to listen to.

DAY 10 CHALLENGE 🎧　　　　⏱ 15 mins

If you listen to this melody, you'll realize there are a few places where the word setting isn't great. <u>Rewrite it to improve its prosody</u> – the way its words and music fit together.

Let's be honest: there's some pretty bad word setting here. So you've got your work cut out.

A great first step with this challenge is to speak the lyric out loud. (There's a words-only version on the next page if it helps.) The key to good prosody is capturing the stresses, rhythms and melodic rises and falls of natural speech – so the way you'd naturally speak these words is always going to be your best guide for does and doesn't work well.

From there, you'll want to play, sing or listen to the recording of the melody, and listen out for any spots where the melody is distorting the natural way someone would say those words. (And boy, there are some clangers.)

Again, there are three things you're particularly listening out for:

1) Places where the natural syllable stresses of each word in the lyric don't land on the downbeats – in this case beats 1 and 3 – of the music. (Quick hint: there's really only one example of this in the melody – it's kind of subtle and is somewhere around the middle.)

2) Places where the melody's rhythm distorts the natural speech rhythm of any phrase in the lyric, at least enough that sounds weird. (There are a few of these.)

3) Places where a long or high note puts an emphasis on a word that doesn't deserve it. (The setting of the chorus's lyrical hook 'So cold' seems natural – and is especially nice in how it draws out those long 'oh' vowels. The little echoes in parentheses seem to work pretty well also. But there are a few moments where a long or high note emphasizes a word that's not important or emotionally loaded at all, and it sounds unnatural.)

Once you've done that, try and find better solutions for the problem moments you've identified. It's totally up to you what changes you make, but it's possible to improve this melody mostly by changing only its rhythm. There are at least a couple of places where you'll want to change one or more pitches as well, but I'll leave it up to you to decide what's best.

Now, in all of my 30-Day Challenges I have a 'no answers at the back of the book' policy, because the challenges are all about the solutions *you* come up with, not me. But in this case – and since this three-page mega challenge already seems to be breaking all of the rules – I'm going to make an exception.

So when you're done – and definitely only when you're done – if you head right to the back of the book you can check out one solution that significantly improves the prosody of the melody in this challenge. (Though of course it's just one solution – yours might be just as good, only different.)

SO COLD

Why'd you gotta be so cold? (So cold)

Yeah, your heart's like ice.

So cold, (So cold)

No, you don't play nice.

Gimme a sign if you're mine,

If you're not you gotta set me free. (Set me free)

Cuz you're so cold, (So cold)

This game ain't any fun for me.

[DAYS 11–12]
THE CHORD
PROGRESSION
STARTER

[DAYS 11–12]

THE CHORD PROGRESSION STARTER

Nice work – you're steaming ahead and have hit the first of the longer challenges. To kick off with something fairly straightforward, today you're going to craft a complete chorus – with a groove and vocal melody – given a set of chords to work with.

As you probably know, you can start building a song with pretty much any part of it, but a chord progression is always a solid choice. While your song's grooves might be its heart and soul, chord progressions can be a great foundation for building a complete musical texture, and for mapping out a song bar by bar.

> **Why it matters:** Mapping out a chord progression and building the other elements of your song on top of it can be a very effective way of constructing each of your song's sections.

DAYS 11–12 CHALLENGE 30–60 mins

Write a complete chorus – melody, groove, everything except the lyric – given this 16-bar chord sequence:

I Em	I F	I Am	I G	I
I Em	I F	I Am	I G	I
I C	I Em	I Am	I Am/G	I
I F	I G	I C	I	I

First things first – play or listen to the chord progression to get a feel for how it sounds. The progression is in C major but starts on an E minor chord – and only features one C major chord before coming to rest on one at the end – so it has a fairly unsettled feel.

From there, you'll want to make decisions about the tempo, style and feel you want your song to have. And while this challenge isn't about working with a lyric, you might want to suggest a title – or at least a vague idea of what the song's message is – to help you write something that conjures up a particular vibe or mood.

Then, focus on either tackling the song's melody or groove. Start small if you need to – figuring out a melody over simple held chords, then constructing a groove underneath that once you're done. As always, let your instincts guide you – try things out, keep hold of anything you like, and keep trying new things until you're done.

[DAYS 13–14]
THE BUILD
CHALLENGE

[DAYS 13-14]

THE BUILD CHALLENGE

There are lots of different ways to build an effective verse-chorus structure, but pretty much every example is based on one simple principle: the chorus is the song's main event, and the verse and anything else that goes with it anticipates and builds into each chorus.

That means virtually every verse-chorus structure is made of verse-chorus cycles that rise and fall, building up and into each chorus. That's one a way song structures hold their audience's attention – they make their listeners feel like something exciting is coming long before it actually hits.

Today you're going to try putting this idea into practice – focusing on the way you can use a verse build to keep your song engaging.

> **Why it matters:** The key to making a verse-chorus structure work is creating an effective rise and fall in each verse-chorus cycle: that's one important way to keep your song interesting and your audience hooked.

DAYS 13–14 CHALLENGE

 30–60 mins

Choose one of the grooves you wrote on Days 1 or 4 and craft it into a full 16-bar verse groove. Make sure the verse builds effectively in its second half to anticipate and prepare for the chorus that would come after it.

This challenge is all about energy levels – setting up a core groove or feel in the first half of the verse, then building on it to make things more exciting. There are tons of ways you can do this – including making the groove busier and more energetic, using more unusual harmonies, thickening the texture and making the sound louder overall.

Use any of these tools however you like to create that sense of anticipation or build in preparation for an imaginary chorus. At a minimum, take your chosen groove, spin it out over a 16-bar chord sequence and focus on how you can subtly vary it in the second half to create a sense of building. You can include a vocal melody if you want to, but that's definitely optional.

If you have some experience doing this already and want a tougher challenge, consider writing a verse and pre-chorus together – a distinct section that builds from the verse into the chorus that follows it. If you do, you'll want to write new chords and create a new groove – one that's distinct from the verse groove but related to it somehow – for the moment you reach the pre-chorus.

But however you do it, this challenge is all about creating a build – a sense of anticipation that makes us excited for the chorus.

49

[DAY 15–16]
THE LYRIC SETTING
CHALLENGE

[DAYS 15–16]

THE LYRIC SETTING CHALLENGE

Pretty high on the list of 'Most annoying things songwriters get asked at parties' is the age-old question 'Does the music or the lyric come first?'. And as you might know, there's no right answer – as long as they both fit together in the end, it doesn't matter which came first.

Still, as a songwriter it's important to be able to write music to a lyric that a co-writer might have given you or that you wrote yourself.

Part of this challenge is just about combining a well-written melody, chord progression and groove into an effective whole. But just as important is making musical choices that fit the mood or message of the lyric you're working with so that all of the parts of the song work together to create the same overall effect. So let's do it.

Why it matters: Writing music to fit a draft lyric given to you – or that you wrote yourself – is an important songwriting skill.

DAYS 15–16 CHALLENGE

 30–60 mins

Write a complete chorus with this lyric:

MY FAVORITE MISTAKE

'Cos you're my favorite mistake,

My favorite mistake,

No way I'll regret this

In the end.

Yeah, you're my favorite mistake,

My favorite mistake,

And one I'd make

Again and again and again.

As I said, there are two parts to this challenge: writing music that works on its own terms, and writing music that matches and supports the lyric in front of you. So think about how the musical choices you're making – the melody, groove and chords you decide on – fit well with the overall vibe and message of this lyric.

This is a draft lyric, so if you want to tweak some of the details to make it work for the musical ideas you have in mind, you're welcome to make those changes. (In real life, you'd want to run any changes by your co-writer. But in this case your co-writer is me, and you have my pre-approval to do what you like.)

[DAYS 17–18]
MELODY REWRITE

[DAYS 17–18]

MELODY REWRITE

Way back in the days of the quick challenges, you did some specific rewriting assignments – you improved the counterpoint between a melody and its bassline, and revised a vocal melody to improve its prosody. But more generally in songwriting – in both the real world and in these challenges – rewriting is a really essential skill songwriters have to develop.

As the saying goes, great songs aren't written but rewritten. Great songs almost never spill out in a flash of perfect inspiration – their first drafts usually come out promising but not great just yet, and they need plenty of tweaking, editing and polishing to make them shine.

Rewriting can be tough, but it's really as simple as finding parts of a draft that could be better, then figuring out specific ways to fix them. And in today's melody rewriting challenge that's exactly what you're going to do.

> **Why it matters:** Writing your best songs means being comfortable rewriting, editing and tweaking your initial ideas until they become great.

DAYS 17–18 CHALLENGE   ⏱ 30–60 mins

Spend 30–60 minutes improving this chorus vocal melody:

You'll see a vocal melody that's kind of sort of OK, but has a couple of gaps and could definitely be improved. Rewrite whatever you like – including the lyric if you want – but in particular there are a few places the melody feels boring or weird and the rhythm is a bit square. Think of this melody as a first draft you might have scribbled down, and now it's your job to make it the best melody you can.

[DAYS 19–20]
BUILDING BRIDGES

[DAYS 19–20]

BUILDING BRIDGES

The challenges so far have focused on crafting verses and choruses, so today you're going to think about writing another important song section: the bridge.

If a verse-chorus structure includes a bridge, it almost always comes after the second chorus, to create a V-C-V-C-B-C overall structure. That's a great place for a bridge because it breaks up the regular pattern of alternating verses and choruses, and takes the song – and its audience – somewhere new. And, in a nutshell, that's exactly what a bridge does: creates a diversion, or a distraction or just a quick escape to somewhere fresh.

It's worth keeping that idea in mind, because it's the crux of completing today's challenge.

Why it matters: Being able to craft bridges that take us somewhere fresh and diversionary is an essential songwriting skill.

DAYS 19–20 CHALLENGE

 30–60 mins

Take the music you wrote on Days 15–16 and <u>write the music to an 8-bar bridge that could come immediately after that chorus</u>.

Again, the key to writing a successful bridge – both musically and lyrically – is to create a section that takes us somewhere your song hasn't been yet. Musically that usually means fresh chords and a fresh melody – maybe in a slightly different vocal register, or part of the voice – but mostly a fresh feel overall.

In fact, if you listen to the bridges in plenty of your favorite songs you'll notice that musically they often feel floaty or ethereal – like a diversion or escape, as I said – so that's a character worth trying to capture if you can.

Assume that this bridge is going to come directly after the song's second chorus and lead directly into the song's third and final chorus. So you'll also want to map out chords that are different from the chorus, but also lead effectively back to the chorus's beginning.

This is a musical challenge, so you don't need to think about writing or setting a specific lyric. Still, you're welcome to sketch out some phrases or an overall idea for the bridge lyric if that helps you focus on creating effective music for it.

[DAYS 21–22]
GROOVE REWRITE

[DAYS 21–22]

GROOVE REWRITE

Alrighty – you're into the twenties and making great progress. And today it's another challenge that's so epic it can't be contained by the usual single-page challenge format.

From Day 1, we've talked about how important finding a great groove is in a new song, and how important the mood or emotional temperature a groove creates is to the song's overall effect.

As it turns out, that's a really subtle art. You can make small changes to a groove – an extra note, a tweaked rhythm, a different sound or instrument – and end up with a strikingly different effect. And the more distinctive, specific and even detailed you make a groove, the more memorable and effective it tends to be.

The trouble is, your first attempt at a groove will often come out over-simple, over-familiar or even clichéd. And while that can work sometimes, it's also important to be able to take a basic or well-worn groove pattern and develop or refine it into something really great.

Why it matters: The art of groove writing is the art of writing something that captures your song's big idea musically, but still sounds fresh and individual.

DAYS 21–22 CHALLENGE   30–60 mins

Rewrite these three grooves to make them sound more individual and distinctive:

[1]

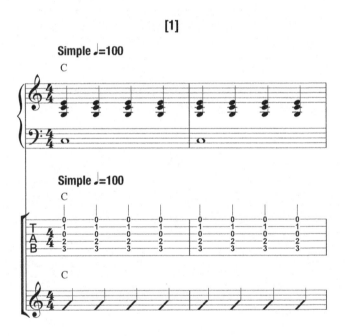

[2]

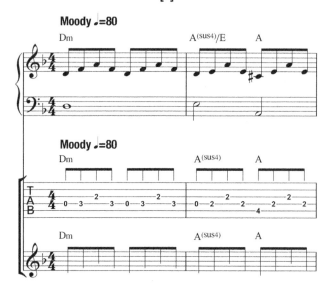

[3]

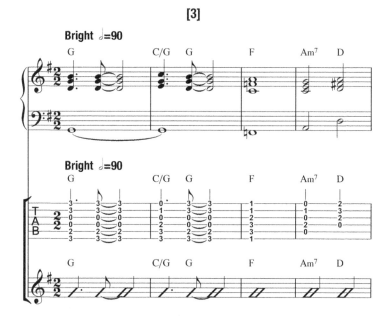

THE 30-DAY MUSIC WRITING CHALLENGE

Rewrite or refine literally anything about these grooves that you want – their rhythms, chords, keys, figuration, tempos, anything – and add or take away any element as you like. Like you did in the melody challenge, think of these grooves as first drafts – and now see how interesting and irresistible a bit of rewriting can make them.

If it helps, pick a mood or emotion you want to capture – determined, heartbroken, ecstatic, cautious, whatever – and see if that guides you toward some specific changes. You could also come up with a song title or key lyric phrase if that helps you create a particular mood or overall effect.

30–60 minutes is more than enough time to get stuck in with this challenge, so don't be afraid to experiment – you've got time to try out plenty of ideas for each groove before settling on anything. There's plenty of room to add detail, but – as I said – sometimes making even one small but decisive change can turn an unremarkable groove into a really exciting one.

Finally, you'll notice with each groove I've given you two versions – a piano/synth version and a guitar version. They're not strictly identical, but they represent the same musical idea or intention on keys and then guitar. So pick whichever version you want to start with, depending on what instrument or instruments you're writing for, and see what magic you can conjure up with them.

And if you finish up in less than 30 minutes, you're always welcome to write more variations or versions of the three basic grooves to fill the time.

[DAYS 23–24]
INTROS AND OUTROS

[DAYS 23-24]

INTROS AND OUTROS

A song's intro and outro – if it has them – form its outer edges. And while both sections are usually only a few measures long, they're how you get your audience in and out of your song, so they're worth writing well.

In a verse-chorus structure that means the job of most intros is to set up – musically in particular – the song's first verse, and the job of most outros is to round off the song's last chorus. (Check out Appendix 2 if you need more information about how these two sections typically fit within an entire verse-chorus structure.)

There are tons of ways you can create effective intros and outros, but today you're going to practice crafting them based on a few popular, tried-and-tested formats.

Why it matters: Being able to write good intros and outros is an essential part of writing great songs.

DAYS 23–24 CHALLENGE

 30–60 mins

Write <u>three different intros that lead into one of the grooves you came up with on Days 1 or 4.</u> (Stick with the same groove each time.) Then write <u>three different outros that could follow the chorus you wrote on Days 11–12.</u>

That might sound like a lot of writing, but it's not, I promise, because I'm going to give you a few specific techniques to try.

First, try writing an intro that's just four extra measures of your verse groove that prefigure the moment your verse arrives. Ditto, try an outro that extends your chorus groove for a few measures then stops. (Both these techniques are very simple but get used a lot.)

Second, try writing an intro that's similar to but not exactly like your first verse's groove – maybe it foreshadows or anticipates it in some way, or maybe it's a bit busier but settles down for the first verse. Ditto, try an outro that extends your chorus groove but is decidedly different from it somehow.

Finally, try writing an intro and an outro that are original, or 'through-composed' – definitely different from the sections they lead into or extend out of. In this case you'll probably want to use some elements from the main body of the song so the sections don't just feel weirdly tacked on, like they're from another song. You can get creative here – but again, try to create something that fits.

If you get through all three intros and all three outros with tons of time to spare, feel free to write some more.

[DAYS 25–26]
ONE OF A KIND

[DAYS 25–26]

ONE OF A KIND

One thing pretty much every great artist has in common is that they have a sound that's completely their own. Whether it's The Beatles, The Killers or The Weeknd, their music has a distinctive sound that makes it – if you know what to listen out for – instantly recognizable.

In fact, one of the hallmarks of great songwriting is when a song, album or EP becomes so individual that it makes you forget temporarily that any other song exists. And the way to do that what you create is by trying to write the song only you can write – to make each song new by making it specific to you, and original enough that it creates its own uniquely captivating musical world.

That's no small task, but it basically comes down to embracing all the things that make you different or weird as a musician – the ideas, influences and sounds you love – and using them shamelessly in everything you write. That's what you'll do today.

> **Why it matters:** Whatever it is that makes you unique – your tastes, your influences, your favorite sounds – are exactly the sort of things you should embrace to make your music sound unique.

DAYS 25–26 CHALLENGE

 30–60 mins

List three to five musical things – sounds, chords, instruments, melodic shapes, instrumental techniques, ideas, styles and/or genres – that you find really interesting or fun. Then write an 8- or 16-bar chorus that incorporates all of them.

So you've figured out what makes this challenge work – it's about embracing whatever it is that makes you and your musical tastes distinctive and trying to incorporate them all in a single song section.

It's up to you whether you include a melody in what you create – that's a good idea, but most important is that you craft some music, even just a groove, that shows off the handful of musical elements that get you most fired up.

Maybe it's a specific kind of guitar or piano figuration. Maybe it's a specific synth sound in a DAW. Maybe it's an extended guitar technique – like harmonics or hitting the strings percussively. Maybe it's a specific type of chord, a specific rhythm, or just an overall sound that's ultra poppy or sounds like textbook R&B or country or EDM or any other genre. Either way, try to embrace it and include it in what you write.

As usual, if coming up with song title, concept or message for this chorus helps you write, then go ahead. Your goal is to combine all of these disparate elements into a coherent whole. If you do, chances are what you write will sound completely unique – and that means you're doing this challenge exactly right.

[DAYS 27–28]

THE

REHARMONIZATION

CHALLENGE

[DAYS 27–28]

THE REHARMONIZATION CHALLENGE

Today's challenge is another rewriting challenge and another chord progression challenge. But unlike the previous chord progression challenges, you don't have the freedom to write whatever you feel like. Instead, you're going to spend some time reharmonizing a melody that's already been written.

It's a useful skill to practice – both for harmonizing finished melodies that you have in front of you and for revisiting chord progressions you've already written to see if you can turn them into something even more interesting, or just different.

Why it matters: Being able to harmonize or reharmonize a melody quickly is an essential songwriting skill.

DAYS 27–28 CHALLENGE   30–60 mins

Rewrite the harmonies of this 16-bar chorus melody:

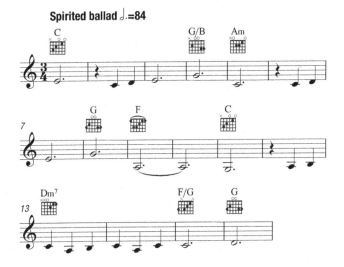

As you'll see, you've got a simple 3/4 melody with maybe a 90s R&B boy band feel to it – and plenty of ways to harmonize it.

So play around with whatever harmonic vocabulary you have and find something you like the sound of. If in doubt, try switching out chords, using inverted (slash) chords, adding a handful of sevenths or adding or removing some of the chord changes.

If you finish with plenty of time to spare, you can repeat the 16-bar melody to make this a 32-bar challenge. If you do, change or vary the chords again – even subtly – on the repeat, and you'll probably want to alter the melody the second time so it finishes on C.

[DAYS 29–30]
THE COVER
CHALLENGE

[DAYS 29–30]

THE COVER CHALLENGE

Great work – you've made it to the final challenge. And as promised, I saved you something special for the big finish. Today you're going to write a cover version of one of your favorite songs.

You've already done a handful of rewriting challenges to improve OK material – but today's challenge is different. It's your chance to have some fun recasting and reimagining a song you love in your own way, while bringing together pretty much all of the skills you've developed throughout these challenges.

If you planned ahead and already have a song chosen, that's great. If not, take a quick break to go find the sheet music – or at least the lyrics and chords – of a song you love. Then when you're ready, let's go.

> **Why it matters:** Arranging and reimagining one of your favorite songs is not only a great creative challenge – it's a really fun way of using lots of different songwriting skills at once.

DAYS 29–30 CHALLENGE

 30–60 mins

Write a creative cover of one of your favorite songs.

Pretty much the only rule here is that you should keep the original lyrics intact but take as much creative license as you like to reinvent the groove and chords, and even the melody – provided it keeps the original song recognizable. Just aim to create a cover that's definitely the original song, only a creative new version of it.

One great way to do this is to recast a song you love in a new style. Maybe you've always wondered what a hard rock 'Despacito', a hip-hop 'Summer of '69', or a salsa version of '...Baby One More Time' would sound like. If so, great. Get creating.

Otherwise, you don't have to be so specific – and can just have fun playing around more freely with the material you've got in front of you to see where you could take it.

If the song you've chosen is particularly long, it's fine to focus on just the first two or three minutes – maybe a couple of verses and choruses.

Enjoy.

ALL DONE – SO WHAT'S NEXT?

ALL DONE – SO WHAT'S NEXT?

Congrats – that's all thirty days done. Play a small fanfare. Pat yourself on the back. Treat yourself to something special.

So now – other than the deservedly warm feeling you probably have inside – what happens next?

As always, that's up to you. But, as always, I have a handful of suggestions.

One thing you can do is just to dive into whatever you write next, bringing everything you've practiced in these challenges with you. Maybe you want to put something you discovered about grooves, chords or melodic writing into practice in a real-life song. If so, go ahead. Take those skills even further.

You'll also have plenty of great material on hand you created while completing the challenges, so you could use some of it directly – a groove, a vocal melody, a chord progression – in whatever you write next. In fact, it's worth keeping this book and everything you created with it on hand. Then any time you're feeling stuck or blocked, you can revisit some material you came up with or redo one or two of the challenges to give you new material for a bigger project.

But most of all – whatever you do next – keep writing and keep listening to the music you love. Your best teacher is always the music you love most – and having got through these challenges, most likely you'll be thinking differently about all kinds of songwriting techniques and ideas you hadn't thought much about before. So keep listening out for how your favorite songwriters use these ideas in your favorite songs – that's an education in itself.

If you're looking for new challenges – and didn't realize this book was part of a series – there are other 30-Day Challenges devoted to helping you write better lyrics, finish complete songs and become more creative at everything. There's more information – as well as tons of free resources and articles – on The Song Foundry site.

You could also come back to the challenges in this book in a few months' time and work through them in a different style or with a co-writer to mix things up. Or you could just try each challenge again to see how much smarter and bolder you'll be at tackling them the second time round.

But whatever you choose, and wherever you go next – good luck. Writing songs is one of the most fascinating and rewarding things you can do with your life, and it's been an honor to have shared part of your songwriting journey with you.

So write on, my friend. Go make some noise.

ALSO BY ED BELL: *THE ART OF SONGWRITING*

The Art of Songwriting is a unique songwriting guide that's not about learning rules and following methods, but about **how to think, create and live like a songwriter**.

It covers all the big concepts that go into making great songs – not just the craft of songwriting, but how creativity works and what it means to be an artist.

The Art of Songwriting is available as an eBook at **thesongfoundry.com/ebook** and in paperback online and in bookstores.

[APPENDIXES]

[APPENDIX 1]

CHORDS & GUITAR CHARTS CHEATSHEET

In case they're useful, on the next two pages there's a quick guide to all twelve basic major and minor triads that exist and that you might use when writing a song.

Each chord is shown with the three notes that make up the triad for playing it on a keyboard or DAW, plus a guitar chord diagram to show you the easiest way to play it on a guitar.

The chords are arranged according to their place in the cycle of fifths, so related chords – the ones that you're most likely to use together – are near each other or in the parallel position on the opposite page. So in the key of C major, for example, the chords you're most likely to use are C, F and G as well as Am, Dm and Em.

Where there are two chords right next to each other, it's because they're enharmonic – the same chords, only spelled using different note names.

MAJOR CHORDS

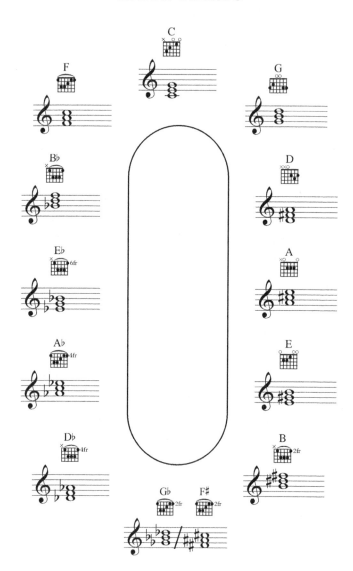

MINOR CHORDS

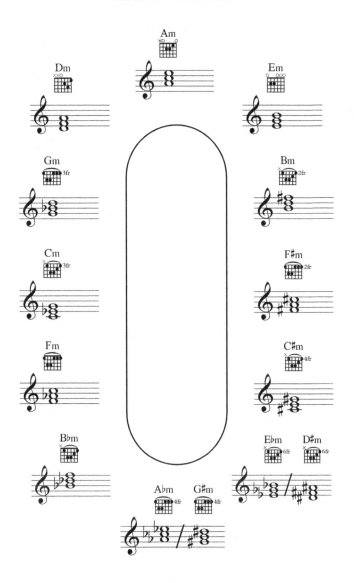

[APPENDIX 2]

VERSE-CHORUS STRUCTURE SUMMARY

Whenever song structure is a factor in this book, the challenges are geared toward building verse-chorus structures because they're by far the most common song structures used today. But to help put some of these challenges in context, on the next page I've given you a table from my book *The Art of Songwriting*, which summarizes how a verse-chorus song structure typically works.

Verse-chorus structures can take lots of different forms and variations, but here's the one that's usually considered the most archetypal or fundamental:

Intro *(optional)*
Verse 1
Chorus 1
Verse 2
Chorus 2
Bridge *(optional)*
Chorus 3
Outro *(optional)*

All of the challenges in this book are based on this archetypal structure, but if you're interested in writing more advanced verse-chorus structures – or some of the other song forms – you can find out more about them in *The Art of Songwriting*.

OPENING	VERSE-CHORUS CYCLES				CONTRAST	RETURN	
Sets up groove and world of song.	*Alternating VERSES and CHORUSES. VERSES set up and build into CHORUSES. Later cycles often varied in subtle or profound ways.*				*Something new and diversionary.*	*Final arrival at CHORUS plus conclusion of song.*	
INTRO	VERSE 1	CHORUS 1	VERSE 2	CHORUS 2	BRIDGE	CHORUS 3	OUTRO
INTRO • No proper lyric yet, but maybe vocal riffing • May be derived from VERSE or CHORUS and/or **CHORUS** • In full or part • Often a 'preview' version, thinned out or altered somehow	**VERSE** • Basic groove • Sets up • Background to song • Around half-way point, often starts to build noticeably in anticipation of CHORUS and sometimes **PRE-CHORUS** • Distinct transitional section • Marked change in lyric direction, harmony or texture as moves towards CHORUS	**CHORUS** • States central idea of song • Most memorable section • Bigger groove, thickest texture or most energy so far and sometimes **TAG** • Maybe gives singer a break with short TURNAROUND, maybe extends CHORUS with POST-CHORUS, or outdoes CHORUS with even bigger DROP	**VERSE** • Shares more background info or detail • Almost always new lyric • May be shorter than VERSE 1 (often half the length) and sometimes **PRE-CHORUS** • Same effect as PRE-CHORUS 1 • Lyric is often identical or very similar to PRE-CHORUS 1	**CHORUS** • Lyric usually identical to CHORUS 1, maybe with minor changes • Sometimes changes in texture to CHORUS 1 and sometimes **TAG** • Same effect as TAG 1 • Texture sometimes changed	Various possibilities: **BRIDGE** • Totally distinct from anything so far • Lyric adds a new perspective and/or **INSTRUMENTAL** Vocal drops out for instrumental solo or maybe dance section and sometimes then **VERSE** or **PRE-CHORUS** or **VERSE & PRE-CHORUS** • Links BRIDGE and final CHORUS • Texture, lyric or length may be altered	**CHORUS** • CHORUS may be repeated • Often something new in instrumental texture, or major vocal riffing added • Lyric usually identical to other CHORUSES, though sometimes minor changes • Final CHORUS often the biggest moment in the song	**SUDDEN STOP** or **REPEAT & FADE** • Chorus repeated and fades out or **OUTRO** • Distinct ending • No proper lyric, though maybe vocal riffing • May be totally new but often derived from CHORUS, VERSE or INTRO

[APPENDIX 3]

GLOSSARY

As I said in the introduction, this book uses a handful of specific musical terms to explain some of the challenges. So if you found yourself unsure or confused about any of them, here's a list of quick definitions – plus a few other important terms I've also put in bold as part of the definitions.

As a humble appendix, there isn't room for a deep dive into any advanced music theory – you'll want to pick up a different book for that – but these definitions will give you a quick introduction or refresher to these fundamental concepts.

Chord

A **chord** is any two or more notes played simultaneously – but in practice most harmony in songwriting revolves around three-note chords called **triads**. The two most fundamental chord types in songwriting are **major** and **minor**, but there are lots of ways to modify these basic chords by adding, removing and/or altering their notes.

Counterpoint

Derived from the Latin phrase *punctus contra punctum*, meaning 'point against point' – **counterpoint** describes the relationship between two or more melodic parts in a musical **texture**. For example, two melodic parts might share the exact same rhythm or have complementary rhythms that interlock in an interesting way. Likewise, two parts might move melodically in **similar motion** – their notes move melodically in the same direction – or in **contrary motion** – in the opposite direction.

Groove

In music generally, a **groove** is the rhythmic feel or sense of drive that a piece or section of music as a whole creates. But in songwriting, a groove is specifically the underlying musical idea, figuration or rhythmic pattern – without the lead vocal – that characterizes a song, or a particular section within it.

A song's groove is usually a unit of maybe one, two or four measures that is repeated and maybe developed throughout a song or song section to form its core instrumental texture. Some grooves include **riffs** – repeated guitar figures – but most feature plenty of repetition of melodic or rhythmic **motifs**.

Hook

In songwriting, a **hook** is any part of a song that's catchy and repetitive enough to be memorable to a listener – something that hooks them in and/or hooks into them. So hooks can be musical – ideas that are repeated over and over so that a listener will remember them – or lyrical – any word or phrase repeated enough times that they're easily remembered.

Key

Most so-called Western music – including most genres of songwriting – is **tonal**, which means it sits in a specific **key** or **tonality**. Each key – such as C major or G minor – has a specific set of **diatonic** notes – the notes that belong naturally in that key – which give different types of keys different qualities. Major keys tend to sound brighter and minor keys more moody or melancholy, for example.

Each key also has its own hierarchy of notes. So for example, in C major the note C is at the top of that hierarchy, so a song will feel most at rest if its vocal part finishes on a C note.

Measure (or Bar)

A **measure** or **bar** is the basic unit of time that rhythms are organized into. The number and type of beats that each measure has is indicated by a **time signature**, and measures are shown in music notation by **bar lines** – vertical lines that indicate the end of one measure and the start of the next.

Meter (or Time Signature)

A song's **meter** or **time signature** is a sign made up of two numbers that indicate how many beats are in each measure of a piece of music, and what the basic rhythmic unit of those beats is. For example, **4/4** – the most common meter in songwriting – means there are four quarter notes (or crotchets) in each measure.

Other common meters include **3/4** (three quarter notes per bar), as well as **compound meters** such as **6/8** and **12/8** (six and twelve eighth notes per measure respectively) in which each beat consists of three eighth notes grouped together, instead of the usual groups of two in **simple meters,** like 4/4 or 3/4.

Motif

A **motif** – sometimes spelt '**motive**' – is a short musical idea that is characterized by a distinctive melodic shape or contour – a melodic motif – or sometimes just by a distinctive rhythm – a rhythmic motif. Motifs are important because they're the building blocks of great melodies – good melodic writing is about repeating and developing one or more motifs into a coherent whole.

Prosody

In songwriting, **prosody** describes the relationship between a song's lyric and its vocal melody. When spoken, every word has a natural stress pattern (like 'to-MOR-row') and most phrases come with a loose rhythm and a melodic rise and fall. Good prosody is about making sure the melody that goes with a song lyric follows these patterns – or at least doesn't distort them in a weird or unnatural way.

Scale

A scale is a series of notes moving up or down stepwise, with neighboring note names. There are dozens and probably hundreds of different types of scale, but the two most important in songwriting, by far, are the **major scale** and the **minor scale**. Each **key** has a specific scale, which contains the most important (and usually most common) melodic notes used by music written in that key. The individual notes of a scale are often referred to as **scale degrees** – so, for example, the fourth scale degree in a C major scale is F.

Slash Chord

A **slash chord** is a chord whose bass note is any note other than the chord's **root** (the note in the chord name). So, for example, in a C major chord, the bass or lowest note is ordinarily a C. But in a slash chord such as C/E or C/D, the bass note is an E or D – below the usual C major chord of C, E and G – instead.

The most common type of slash chord is an **inverted chord**, where one of the chord's notes other than the root is in the bass – like C/E. But sometimes, like in C/D, the bass note isn't a note that appears elsewhere in the chord.

Structure (or Form)

A song or any piece of music's **structure** or **form** describes the way the piece of music is organized in time: the sections that make up the piece of music, and how those sections return and repeat.

Common song sections include the **verse**, **pre-chorus**, **chorus**, **bridge**, **intro** and **outro** – and there's more information about how they all work in a **verse-chorus structure**, the most common song form, in Appendix 2.

Syncopation

A **syncopated** or **off-beat** rhythm is a rhythm with many notes that don't land on a song's main beats. Syncopated rhythms tend to sound more exciting, cool or funky – and less square – than on-beat rhythms, so they're used a lot in songwriting.

Tempo

A song's tempo is its speed. There are two common ways to indicate a song's tempo, and at least in printed sheet music they're often used together. One is to describe the tempo – or the overall mood – in words, like 'fast', 'steady' or 'slowly'. (Italian words are sometimes used also, following the convention in classical music.) The other is to specify the tempo with what's called a **metronome mark**, like "♩=120", which means the quarter note (or crotchet) is the basic unit of the song's beat, and there are 120 beats per minute, or bpm.

Texture

Texture describes the number of musical parts a piece of music, or a section within a piece of music, has – and the relationship between them. So the texture of a song would be described as thicker if it has a lot of instruments or tracks playing, or thinner if it has only one or two playing. Similarly, a texture would be described as busy if the parts or tracks have a lot of rhythmic activity, or simple or sparse if the parts have only held chords.

Vocal Range

Vocal range refers to the maximum **interval** – the musical distance – between the highest and lowest note in a song or piece of music. It's an important characteristic to bear in mind, as most singers are limited in the notes they can comfortably sing, depending on their voice type. The vocal range for most songs is a **tenth**, or ten notes of the scale, but a lot of songs stick within an **octave**, or eight notes of a normal major or minor scale.

Vocal Register

Vocal register refers to the part of the vocal range any particular section of a song is in – so, for example, you might say a song's chorus is in a higher vocal register, or part of the voice, than its bridge. The word **register**, on its own, can also refer to part of an instrument's range – for example, you might describe a clarinet's low register as thick and woody and its high register as more shrill.

For more tools, ideas and inspiration,
visit **thesongfoundry.com**

One possible solution to The Prosody Challenge:*

Made in the USA
Monee, IL
16 March 2021